WORK
WITHOUT STRESS AND OVERCOME BAD HABITS

Discover How to Develop Motivation, Increase Productivity, Declutter Your Mind and Relieve Anxiety

Full Mindset

CHAPTER ONE

Working With Difficult People

The thing with difficult people is that they have been everywhere for as long as this world can remember. They may not have been as prevalent in the past, way back when there were fewer people, and everyone was so segregated. But life, as we know it, is getting more and more crowded, and populations are not getting less dense anytime soon. This is why, now more than ever, we need to start learning how to cope with them.

While it doesn't take a genius to tell what makes a person so difficult, sometimes we do need a bit of help spotting them. Being a victim of difficult people yourself, you often get into the heat of things, unable to take on the right mindset for the task. Knowing a few cues could help you snap back to reality and be able to tell yourself "Hey, I need to deal with this person."

Of course, complaints from another person are the best way to spot a difficult person. When you hear other people complain about what someone you know did or said, it's obviously because they're not getting along well, and that could be because somebody is being difficult. When you yourself find that you're better off without a specific person around or you want to minimize contact with that person, then you may be dealing with a difficult person, but you just haven't learned how to deal with him or her yet.

- In a nutshell, difficult people are the kind who: are hard to deal with or to satisfy;

- make you feel tense; make you feel awkward;

- don't understand most conversations;

- don't seem to enjoy the company of others; don't take criticism well.

Yes, I know who these people are, so what's the problem?

There doesn't seem to be, does it? But that's because identifying difficult people is the easiest part. You're probably at this stage right now, but if not, try to imagine having to deal with these difficult people on a daily basis. That means at some point of your day you get to feel uncomfortable or stressed because of somebody else.

The reality is that no person is ever an island. We are all social creatures who need other people in order to survive. Ideally, we have to get along with these people, not because we want to but because we need to.

Imagine these scenarios:

- You need to be patient with your boss, who might have the habit of taking out his stress on you;

- You make lots of friends with whom you must strike some compromise so you don't end up in conflict with someone or you don't get caught in the middle of two other people;

- You have no choice but to put up with some relatives or other family members;

- You have to relate with people you don't really know or understand, like the mean people who take your orders at the coffee shop or the driver who took your parking spot.

If your idea of coping with these people is to avoid them altogether, you're looking to just live in a cave - forever. As long as you consider yourself a civilized individual, you will have to meet, go through them if you must, in order to get somewhere or accomplish something.

Why can't I just let them have it? They deserve it anyway

Because you're better than that. True, you might get some silent approval if you punch that obnoxious officemate that everybody hates in the face, but do you really want to be that kind of person?

We've come a long way since refraining from using aggression or violence to resolve conflicts. Doing what you imagine yourself doing to a person you hate so much is just going to make you look like the bad guy.

Well, there's also the part where you could get fired or end up in jail. Plus, the aggression, verbal, physical, or otherwise, could incite retaliation, which could get you into even more trouble. But, even if you could get away with what you did, aggression is simply not the way to go. Maybe it can be done as a last resort, but even then, you have to be very discerning about option.

Can I just ignore most of them then?

Probably not. At least not in this day and age. Ignoring someone is considered as passive aggression, which is only slightly less bad than its more direct counterpart, so the risks are pretty much the same.

Sometimes the mere thought of the difficult person can be

the source of your stress. And given how our world has modernized in a way that it's so easy to get in touch with each other, you're going to be getting those thoughts a lot.

Today, people can reach you by phone literally anywhere, and perhaps the only acceptable excuse for not being able to get back to them (aside from when you're sleeping), is when you're driving or when you're in the bathroom. It's even hard to ignore messages from Facebook because they can tell if you've "seen" it.

In short, society makes it so hard for you not to participate in this very connected world that we live in today. Should you choose to ignore these demands, that's going to fall on you more than it will on the difficult person you chose not to deal with.

So, the takeaway from all this is:

- The fight or flight mechanism (i.e. aggression or avoidance) doesn't work;

- Difficult people in the world are harder to get rid of in general, given the highly connected world;

So how do we deal with them?

The secret is Emotional Quotient or EQ. This refers to the capacity of a person to understand not only oneself, but others as well. Having good EQ means you are able to better deal with other persons regardless of whether they are difficult or not. It's basically what determines a person's social abilities.

Emotional Intelligence includes the following skills:

- Identifying your own emotions;

- Exercising self-restraint of your feelings, thoughts, and even actions;

- Active self-awareness, especially when dealing with other people;

- Identifying the current emotional state of other people;

- Being able to sustain good relations with other people; and overall emotional strength and competence.

These are things that can't always be taught directly, but consistently learning how to relate with people and being mindful of how you respond to them is a good way to start. As mentioned before, it takes practice. And given that coping with difficult people is the way to go, developing one's emotional intelligence is a good way to start.

Identifying Difficult People

It was established earlier that difficult people generally make you feel uncomfortable or uneasy. But the truth is that there is no single personality that defines all difficult people. As much as no two people are exactly alike, no two difficult people will fit into a single description.

They do, however, have certain commonalities.

This allows certain types of difficult people, regardless of certain differences, to fall into a set of categories.

For the purposes of this guide, there are four main types of difficult people, namely:

1. The self-centered. These are the people who are difficult because they force others to look at no one else but themselves. They think of no one else but themselves. They fear being ignored and look at others who get attention with bitterness.

2. The control freaks. These people like to have things their way no matter what. They believe they are smarter than anyone else around them, and do not look kindly to rejection. They are difficult because they are hard to compromise with.

3. The disruptor. Their brand of being difficult lies in their ability to just slow down and delay everything. They do this in many ways: they show up late, if at all, they nitpick minor details; they lack the confidence to make decisions. While they may not be as aggressive as the self-absorbed or controlling, they tend to be irritating in their own right.

4. The toxic. These are the people who are downright evil, albeit short of being criminal. The best way to define their brand of difficulty is that they love seeing other people suffer. These are the ones who have the potential to be the most violent or aggressive.

You will notice that most of these classifications resemble personality disorders. This is only natural because these personalities would not be considered disorders if they had no negative effect on other people. But what's important to note is that the source of the difficult personality doesn't matter. Whether the attitude is acquired or genetic, they nonetheless make you feel uncomfortable.

Self-centered: Me, Myself, and I

To the self-absorbed, everything is about him or her, not because it actually is so, but because it has to be. Otherwise, that person would hardly take interest in anything. They possess the symptoms of the narcissist.

They essentially experience the excessive need to care for themselves. While it may be good, if not necessary, to love oneself, the self-centered do this to the extent that they think of no one else. They feel special, and like to make themselves known as such to others. They feel entitled to special treatment, and don't enjoy having to do things they think reduce them to the level of others.

They are generally greedy and needy, but they manifest this in different ways. Some people are straightforward proud and grandiose, towering over others in conversations and saying things to make themselves important.

Others, on the other hand, express really low self-esteem in order to attain affirmation from others. They consistently do things that will make others tell them they are special instead of them making the claim themselves.

Self-centered people become such because of various reasons, but this is largely a result of terrible experiences that cause them to be deprived of their self-esteem. This could be because they were raised by self-centered parents. Or, maybe in the past they were heavily taken for granted or abused. It's a coping mechanism gone wrong, where a person feels the need to have the world compensate for their lost self-esteem.

They tend to become aggressive or irritating when they are not given the recognition, they think they deserve. They tend to hate people who disagree with them and develop aggression towards those who criticize them. They are not always the most talented, but they will never admit that.

Remember that self-centered people value their self-esteem. This means that they need other people to affirm them. Knowing how to make them feel that they are being abandoned could help them realize that they need to mellow down their excessive self-love. If you are able to take control of that aspect of your personality, you can possibly win them over.

Control Freaks: My Way or the Highway

At some point in your life, you've probably experienced having plans not going the way you imagined them. It makes you feel bad, but then you just try to understand why it happened and learn from the experience.

That doesn't cut it for the control freak. To them, not getting their way means that everyone should be punished for being incompetent. To them, anyone who does things differently from how they would have done it is incompetent. They are afraid of spontaneity and anything that doesn't come from them.

They are different from self-absorbed individuals in a sense that they don't always make it about them. To them, it doesn't matter how things are done, as long as they are done in the way the control freak imagined it.

But much like the self-absorbed, the control freak possesses symptoms of narcissism. Their self-esteem, however, is more specific because it targets the output of his or her plans or decisions and their ownership thereof. They became this way because of how they grew up or were raised. Perhaps they were accustomed to being depended on, or maybe they experienced that one time where they trusted someone who had failed them. Because of these experiences, they don't want to take the risk of having to let others take control.

They are also very addicted to power. After all, that's how they are able to take control. This addiction will cause them to compete with others to very notorious extents. These people are talented with bringing other people down, specifically those they think are a threat to their authority.

Control freaks do their thing in different ways. Some of them are very direct in a sense that they will threaten people around them if they don't get what they want. Some of them are very deceptive, getting what they want by manipulating people. Some assert their superiority over others so that they will give in to the controller's demands. Others will be passive, where they don't do anything that they don't think should be done, even when they promised to do so.

Control freaks don't thrive in the presence of people who feel self-sufficient. If you can manage to make them feel indispensable, they lose their power over you.

Disruptor: Always Getting in the Way

At the very least, they will be annoyances. But sometimes they can ruin entire operations, if not your entire day. When something goes wrong, they will be to blame, and no one will disagree.

But what makes disruptors so different from the narcissistic self-absorbed people and the controllers, as well as the huge toxic people is that they work in small increments.

At first, they all seem like small, possibly innocent quirks until you start to see how much they are getting in the way of everybody's job.

It will never be their intention to delay your progress. The disruption is but a byproduct of what they are more concerned with.

They come in many forms. There are pessimists, who refuse to push through with plans, thinking they'll never work. You also have your perfectionists who nitpick every detail that nothing ever gets done in the end. There are also the indecisive and the procrastinators, who either take forever to make a choice or do something they've decided to do.

There are many reasons why disruptors do what they do. It could be due to a lot of negativity or insecurity. It could also be because they don't feel any sense of urgency or are too confident in their skills. This is why dealing with them can be a bit tricky. The general strategy, however, is to just make sure things are done - with or without them.

The Toxic: Everybody's Nightmare

If the world has real live villains, it would be them. These are people who literally revel in the suffering of others. They can be as typical as the rumor mongers or as dastardly as the power-tripping monsters you meet everywhere. These people look as if they were born to do nothing but cause havoc in other people's lives.

Their most insidious trait, however, is the fact that they are highly contagious. If you're not careful, you could fall for their lies about someone and actually hate someone else for the wrong reasons. Their rage could be transferred to you, and you end up being angry at other people as well. This is how the toxic people win.

Of all types of difficult people, this one is probably the most familiar to you. They're the people who make bad, tactless remarks. They're the people who take things too seriously. They are bullies. They are people who have an utter lack in EQ.

Fortunately, what toxic people consider to be their greatest weapon is actually their weakness. Because their behavior is often inexcusable, they are easier to deal with or at the very least, identify. While confronting them shouldn't be the solution, it's quite easy for you to prepare yourself for them.

For instance, simply not taking these people seriously can do wonders.

Let them pass by, make their noise, and then just get on with your day. Depending on your situation, there are many variations to this defensive technique, and you must master them to fully conquer the toxic individual.

CHAPTER TWO

Building Up A Productive Mindset

Having a productive mindset is vital to completing more. Think shrewd as opposed to working harder. While a large portion of us realize that we ought to have the correct mindset, we don't know how to accomplish it. What does a productive mindset resemble? Here, we investigate.

- Think Savvy, Work Keen – The Significance Of Your Mood

At the point when you have a productive mindset, you can utilize every one of your assets. You'll boost your endeavors, your vitality, and your time. It isn't tied in with working harder. It isn't tied in with attempting to achieve everything. It isn't even about attempting to complete things as fast as could reasonably be expected. A productive mindset is tied in with benefiting as much as possible from the things you have. It's additionally about appreciating the procedure. With this attitude, you'll think more brilliant and work more intelligent, completing more.

What components does a productive mindset have? Which components do you have to support yourself to turn out to be increasingly productive? Here are probably the best:

- **Interest** – an eagerness to address, investigate, and search out new ideas and thoughts. It's likewise the craving to learn and know more things.

- **Inspiration** – without it, you can't improve or gain ground.

- **Vision** – in the event that you can picture the things you need to accomplish you can concentrate on them better. At the point when you have a reasonable picture in your mind you can endeavor towards those objectives.

- **Basic reasoning** – you have to survey circumstances unbiasedly. Take a gander at all the favorable circumstances and inconveniences at that point make fitting changes.

- **Fearlessness** – accept that you're fit for

accomplishing your objectives. This permits you to accomplish your latent capacity.

- **Perseverance –** a readiness to defeat affliction and deterrents permits you to accomplish your objectives. Try not to permit others' assessments, misfortunes, or conditions to cause you to feel as though you will fail.

- **An uplifting standpoint –** your mentality represents the deciding moment you. With an inspirational demeanor, you can meet any chance head-on.

- **Receptiveness –** in the event that you have a receptive outlook, you can produce creative new thoughts. You additionally become progressively open to new encounters.

- **Parity –** to work appropriately, you have to keep up balance in your life. It's essential to move in the direction of your objectives. Be that as it may, it's similarly critical to energize your batteries every now and then. Propelling yourself too hard just prompts disappointment and burnout.

At the point when you coordinate every one of these components into your manners of thinking, you'll build up a productive mindset. Thus, you'll accomplish your objectives all the more viably.

- Plan Your Day

Arranging is vital to progress. Plan each day at night more. Utilizing daily agendas can assist you with staying productive. They improve your concentration and association.

You can make those rundowns as long or as short as you wish. You may think that it's generally accommodating to keep them to only three or four things. That way, you'll be bound to accomplish those objectives. This will support your psychological prosperity and increment your productivity exponentially. An excessive number of things on a rundown noble motivation you to feel overpowered and confused.

Scribble down your plan for the day each prior night you head to sleep. This gives you a decent beginning to the following day. Rather than sitting around idly concentrating on which errands should be done, you'll be all set.

A plan for the day permits you to catch each errand that comes in. There'll consistently be assignments coming at you. A daily agenda encourages you to organize the ones that should be done first. Therefore, you can focus on the jobs needing to be done. You'll stay away from superfluous interruptions.

Plan for the day likewise gives you greater lucidity and

helps you to find a steady speed appropriately. You won't overlook anything significant.

Additionally, when you confirm things on the rundown, you get a genuine feeling of prosperity and accomplishment. This by itself makes it beneficial drawing one up.

- The "Eat The Frog" Strategy

This strategy may have a peculiar name, however, it's exceptionally helpful. It depends on an idiom by creator Imprint Twain. His thought was that in the event that you eat a live frog each morning, nothing more regrettable can transpire throughout the day. This is an interesting thought, yet it's actual!

Obviously, it doesn't mean eating a genuine frog! The frog here is the most disagreeable errand on the daily agenda that you've drawn up. It's human instinct to attempt to evade horrendous assignments. We're all blameworthy of putting off something that we should do however don't have any desire to do. Regardless of whether it's a call to a troublesome customer or a long and exhausting report, eating the frog is basic.

At the point when you stay away from an unsavory errand, it's consistently on your mind. It prevents you from continuing ahead with different employments that should be finished. It keeps you from centering. You know constantly that the upsetting assignment must be finished. Why put it off? Do it first and get it off the beaten path!

Despite the fact that it's unpleasant to "eat the frog", it will make the remainder of your day simpler. With the hardest undertaking done, you'll have the simpler employments to concentrate on for the rest of your workday.

Make eating the frog a long-lasting propensity. Tackle that significant assignment before you do whatever else. It is difficult to start, however, it'll support your productivity massively.

What do you do on the off chance that you have more than one horrendous errand to handle? The appropriate response is to eat the ugliest one first! Start with the undertaking that is least engaging. Discover the order to begin straight away and to continue on until you've finished the undertaking. It won't be simple. Be that as it may, when you have into this propensity, you'll understand how it has improved your work life. Your productivity will expand colossally, and you'll feel as though you're accomplishing more.

- Dump The Procrastination

We've just referenced how, as people, we're normally

disposed to tarry. While it's ordinary, that doesn't imply that it's alluring. Procrastination can be the passing sound to your productivity. Instead of postponing occupations until some other time, tackle them head-on. This is the place the "eat the frog" strategy becomes an integral factor. Be that as it may, it doesn't simply apply to the least engaging employments. It applies to completely everything in your life. Regardless of whether at work or at home, discarding the procrastination can have an immense effect.

You probably won't feel that procrastination is a significant issue. In case you're putting off reports that should be accomplished for Friday until Thursday evening, is that actually an issue? All things considered, you're completing them on time. All in all, by what means can the deferral sway your general productivity? We should investigate.

Envision it's Monday and you have a crucial report to complete for Friday morning. You realize the report is basic. Nonetheless, it requires heaps of research. You abhor investigating and composing the report. You, accordingly, choose to put it off. You go through the accompanying three days taking a shot at other, less fundamental errands. At the point when Thursday comes around, you understand the report despite everything should be finished. You're caught.

You have loads of other work to do. In any case, you can't chip away at any of them. You have to complete that exploration and the report finished. You should work the entire night to comply with your time constraint. You present the report as required on Friday. Everything's fine. Notwithstanding, take a gander at how it affected your productivity.

You didn't viably invest the energy on Monday and Wednesday. You ought to have apportioned time to each undertaking as per its significance.

Increasingly significant assignments need a longer time spent on them. Spending longer on a less significant errand isn't expanding esteem.

The work is less significant as of now. You've additionally allowed yourself a few days of nervousness, regardless of whether you understand it or not. That report will have been on your mind the entire time. The more drawn out the undertaking is delayed, the more on the edge you become. You wipe out this concern by handling the activity head-on.

Not just that, in spite of the fact that you completed the report on time, it presumably wasn't so much the greatest quality. This implies you're not accomplishing your own best.

You won't dazzle your directors and you won't put yourself in line for advancement.

Obviously, procrastination is an issue, so how would you dispense with it?

- Recognize what you will in general delay on. Is it generally a similar kind of undertaking?

- Inquire as to why you're putting those undertakings off. Test your answers. Is it in light of your capacity? Your emotions? At the point when you comprehend the explanations behind putting the errand off, you'll be better ready to beat them.

- Think of your activity intend to determine the issue. In case you're stressed that you're unequipped for finishing the assignment, take a course, or read about the subject. In case you're inadequate with regards to trust in addressing a customer on the telephone, take a shot at your confidence.

- Dive in. In spite of the fact that it's difficult to venture out carry out the responsibility you're keeping away from, it's basic. The more you do it, the simpler it becomes. It might require some investment, however soon you'll beat the propensity for lingering.

CHAPTER THREE

Setting Up Your Ideal Workplace

It doesn't make a difference how persuaded and centered you are on the off chance that you don't have the apparatuses you need, and the correct condition to accomplish your work in. That is why we're demonstrating how to set up the ideal workplace. In spite of the fact that you may locate your ideal condition to shift somewhat, make changes that work for you until you feel your workplace is Great.

- ERGONOMIC Work Area, Console, AND Seat

On the off chance that your work-at-home employment implies you'll be investing a great deal of energy in the PC, at that point you're certainly going to require an ergonomic work area, console, and seat. In the event that you plan on going through a really long time in your office, at that point, you should do it in comfort. At the point when you are agreeable, at that point you will be increasingly productive.

On the off chance that you not happy in your seat, you'll invest energy (which however as it were minutes one after another could add to hours) endeavoring to locate the ideal the position that doesn't cause your back to hurt sooner or later.

Composing, regardless of whether individuals acknowledge it or not, is no picnic for the hands and wrists. At the point when you don't utilize the best possible stance, which is anything but difficult to overlook, you run the danger of making monotonous movement wounds, causing torment in the fingers, hands, and wrists. Release this for a really long time, and you could wind up with Carpal Passage Condition, something that as a rule requires a medical procedure.

In the event that you don't care for the structure of the ergonomic consoles (they can take a while to become acclimated to) at that point you ought to, in any event, consider a wrist cushion to utilize at the console and mouse. Many mouse cushions accompany gel rests joined to them.

Your work area ought to take into account your seat to be at the best possible stature, and for your screen to be in the best possible good ways from your face. In the event that your work area needs more space to appropriately address this, you'll end up in a clumsy position, which will prompt torment.

Structuring your office in view of ergonomics isn't generally the most expensive powerful choice, particularly in case you're simply beginning. On the off chance that you should cut corners to set aside cash, get the absolute minimum to kick yourself off, and update all that each piece in turn, until your work zone is as agreeable as you can make it.

- Legitimate LIGHTING

Legitimate lighting is critical to your productivity in such a case that you work in a territory that is excessively dim, you will strain your eyes. Stressing your eyes prompts migraines and feeling tired. In case you're working in a situation that is excessively dim, you'll see it in your temperament since you'll feel tired.

The best circumstance is one that utilizes a mix of regular light and fake light. Regular light will help improve your mindset, and it can likewise assist you with saving money on your vitality bills.

On the off chance that conceivable, set up your home office in a room or region of your home where a great deal of characteristic light gets through most of the day, and incline toward counterfeit light as an auxiliary alternative, for when you should work around evening time, or it is shady outside.

Pick a splendor that improves your state of mind. Excessively brilliant, and you'll detect it. On the off chance that it's so dull you can't see, at that point, you have to go for something a piece more brilliant. Minimal bright lights produce a pleasant white light at a part of the wattage of conventional lights.

It's a smart thought to have an overhead light, yet in the event that this isn't feasible for your arrangement, in any event, have a light either around your work area for a devoted errand work, or a corner light close to your work area. Try not to depend entirely on the light from your screen to assist you with checking whether you work around evening time, as this will cause Eye fatigue.

- Calm ROOM/CORNER

In the perfect home office situation, you have an extra room you can commit to your home office. Be that as it may, the truth of your circumstance might be that you just have a limited quantity of room in another room of your home to devote to your home office. While the edge of a room implies you won't have the option to take the Home Office Assessment conclusion, it is absolutely better than working out of a desk area in a corporate office, right?

Any place you set up your office, attempt to make it in the calmest piece of your home. At the point when the earth around you hushes up, you will have the option to concentrate more on the job that needs to be done.

On the off chance that you need to work while viewing the youngsters, the corner may need to be in your family room, so you can see all the movement, and obviously it won't be as tranquil as you'd like, however, there is an answer for that also.

- HEADSET

In the event that you should have the option to shut out commotion from the encompassing room, at that point A headset is an outright lifeline. You can divert on repetitive sound SimplyNoise.com, or music of your decision to shut out the loud interruptions. In the event that you have little kids around, pick utilizing the earphones on one side, so you can even now hear what you have to.

On the off chance that you have more established youngsters, reveal to them that when your headset is on, you're working and ought not to be pestered except if it is a crisis. This is the signal you need, like keeping the workplace entryway shut when you're occupied, to let people around you realize you mean business.

In addition, on the off chance that you have ordinary calls with customers, you can utilize the headset and an administration like Skype to make the calls you need from your PC—sparing on your significant distance bill. In case you're a sorry typist, you can likewise utilize the receiver on the headset for correspondence purposes, utilizing a program to type as you talk.

- Association MATTERS

Being composed will likewise help keep you productive. When everything has a spot and each spot has a thing, you will be unmistakably increasingly productive, since you realize where everything is the point at which you need it, and won't have to sit around idly time searching for something.

How you sort out your home office is up to you. An authoritative framework that works for one individual might possibly work for another. The straightforward truth is that we could compose another book just on home office association, so here are a couple of tips to help send you the correct way:

- Utilize A File Organizer

On the off chance that most of your business is led on the web, you don't really require paper duplicates of everything, so there's no compelling reason to make an envelope for each of your customers. In any case, you ought to make an envelope for contracts, so you have a paper duplicate to allude to simply on the off chance that an issue emerges. Continuously spare your bills, receipts, business cards from contacts, and so forth. Documenting everything will make it simpler to discover when you need it. In the event that you don't think you'll require it, spare it at any rate, in a different record. Clean that random record out once per month, and record everything in it as needs are. You'll love your documenting framework when the time has come to record charges!

- KEEP A PEN AND PAPER Around YOUR Work Area

As advanced as we as a whole are slanted to be, it is consistently a smart thought to have a pen and paper close by to write notes down on varying. This is particularly accommodating in the event that you have a gathering with a customer, and need to take notes on what was talked about? You can type them up and sort out them later on the off chance that it encourages you. Assuming this is the case, it's a smart thought to email them to your customer to ensure everything is clear and you two are in the same spot.

- Sort Out YOUR EMAIL BOX

It's anything but difficult to get overwhelmed with email. The more individuals you work with, and the more pamphlets you pursue, you'll suffocate in a matter of seconds. In the event that you use Gmail, you can name everything as needs are, and even set up channels to naturally, name messages with your customer's name. For example, if your customer's name is Andrew Williams, you can make an email channel so all messages from AndrewWilliams@email.com will be named Joe. At that point, you can peruse and file the message, so later in the event that you ever need to think that it, simply take a gander at Joe's name. Messages can have different names on the off chance that you'd like. While it might require some investment to set up the underlying name structure and channels, you'll spare yourself quite a lot more time later, since you'll have the option to discover things simpler. You can even utilize channels to consequently, move garbage, so you don't need to sit around idly understanding things that aren't important to you.

- Utilize AN ONLINE Record Reinforcement Administration

PC crashes happen constantly. Regardless of whether your hard drive is salvageable, no one can tell when an infection may render your primary PC is pointless for some time. Having an online reinforcement implies you can get to your customer documents and other significant data at whatever point you need to, from any PC you have to.

A few alternatives include:

- Amazon Cloud

- DropBox

- Google Drive

- Carbonite

These stages consider information access from your PC or cell phone, so it's additionally a great method to back up your telephone information. Since we've secured the essentials of setting up your home office for achievement, we'll share our best productivity privileged insights with you!

Solid Schedules For More Noteworthy Productivity

Being increasingly productive beginnings with setting up schedules throughout your life. While a portion of those schedules is revolved around things like being sorted out grinding away, others are progressively close to home. Executing solid schedules throughout your life is critical to progress and accomplishing your own best.

- Resting And Eating – Helping You To Remain Productive

Getting, in any event, seven hours of rest each night is fundamental for both your psychological and physical wellbeing. Sadly, in excess of 30 percent of individuals are neglecting to accomplish this objective. However, the lack of sleep will decrease your proficiency and productivity. You'll commit more errors and won't accomplish your best.

Getting enough rest, then again, improves your state of mind. It likewise diminishes pressure, improves memory, supports inventiveness, and hones center. You'll be better ready to use sound judgment and you'll complete more.

The nature of your rest is likewise significant. In case you're getting nine hours of low-quality rest, that won't be as advantageous as six hours of fantastic rest. To improve your rest quality, you should attempt to clear your mind and set yourself up for rest. Abstain from utilizing any gadget with a screen in the two hours before bed. Oust TV and telephones from the room. Abstain from drinking liquor or eating an overwhelming dinner before bed. Pondering could be a valuable instrument before bed to clear your mind and help you to rest better.

Be that as it may, getting more rest isn't the main thing you can do to set up a sound everyday practice. Eating great is additionally significant for productivity.

The vast majority think the main advantage of smart dieting is to stay away from ailment and to keep up solid bodyweight. However, eating admirably likewise has a significant positive effect on productivity. Why would that be the situation?

- Eating great will build your readiness and vitality levels.

- It improves your safe framework, so you'll take less time off wiped out.

- You'll rest better so you'll have better focus.

- You'll appreciate better emotional well-being and an increasingly inspirational demeanor.

How might you eat all the more soundly to help your productivity?

- Base every supper on bland nourishments.

- Ensure you eat your 5-a-day.

- Expend more fish, particularly sleek fish.

- Eat less sugar and immersed fat.

- Expend less salt.

- Drink at any rate 2 liters of water every day.

- Eat routinely and don't pass up breakfast.

Just as the above tips, there are some brilliant guidelines that you ought to follow.

Abstain from eating low-quality nourishment. This will diminish your readiness. Nourishments high in soaked and trans fats make you lazy. In the interim, nourishments with a high sugar substance may give you a quick jolt of energy, yet you'll encounter an accident a short time later. Sweet, greasy bites might be advantageous, however they could truly harm your productivity.

Deal with how much caffeine you expend. We're regularly enticed to drink some espresso in case we're feeling under-productive. In any case, exorbitant measures of caffeine diminish your productivity. Like sweet tidbits, abundance caffeine gives you a vitality spike before a productivity-constraining accident. The most ideal approach to stay productive for the duration of the day is to devour caffeine with some restraint. Green tea is a superior decision than espresso and will offer you extra medical advantages.

Never pass up breakfast. Regardless of whether you don't feel hungry when you get up, eating encourages you to wake up. A protein shake, cup of juice, or bit of natural product first thing supports your productivity. You ought to pick low GI nourishments for breakfast at whatever point conceivable. Keep away from the sweet breakfast oat or cakes and pick complex sugars like entire grains. This will guarantee you have a consistent vitality source that will assist you with remaining productive until lunchtime.

Eat little dinners often for the duration of the day. This keeps your blood glucose level consistent. Subsequently, you'll have more vitality. On the off chance that you don't eat much of the time, your glucose level will plunge excessively low between dinners. It will likewise make you indulge at mealtimes, causing a glucose level spike.

This makes your vitality level eccentric and will hurt your productivity. Visit, little dinners space out the fuel gracefully for your body all the more equally. You'll feel more invigorated, complete more, and accomplish your own best in all that you do.

Eat littler parts at mealtimes, particularly at lunch. A tremendous feast will cause you to feel lethargic and will decrease your productivity. On a similar note, abstain from eating any food containing tryptophan on an unfilled stomach. Nourishments like poultry, cheddar, milk, and certain fish have high tryptophan levels. These cause you to feel tired in the event that you ingest them on an unfilled stomach.

The best thing to eat on an unfilled stomach is an organic product. Stuffed with complex sugars and fiber, they separate all the more gradually in the body. The organic product can likewise be processed without any problem. This implies you won't feel the exhaustion that happens with huge parts and hard to process snacks.

Albeit a few people stress overeating starches, they aren't really the foe. Indeed, staying away from basic carbs like cakes or white pasta is prudent. Be that as it may, entire grain complex carbs take more time to be processed. This implies the vitality picked up from them gets spread out.

This keeps you productive in the long haul.

While you're pondering what you ought to eat, abstain from having meat at lunch and breakfast. For the most part, meat is high in fat and it's high in protein. This makes it harder to process and will cause you to feel increasingly drained, affecting your productivity.

Attempt to incorporate nourishments like slick fish and nuts in your eating regimen. These are wealthy in omega-3 unsaturated fats which help the synapses solid. They additionally help the body to store carbs as vitality, not fat. Accordingly, you'll be progressively alert during the day. Eating more fiber is additionally a smart thought since it encourages the body to process food consistently and gradually. This keeps vitality levels on a level for better sharpness and productivity.

Remember to consider what you drink as well. Ensure you drink a lot of water, for good wellbeing as well as for better sharpness. Remaining all around hydrated helps supplements that give vitality to travel through the body. It additionally assists with keeping your blood streaming easily so your heart siphons all the more without any problem.

In case you're enticed to drink liquor before bed to improve night's rest, note that it's an impractical notion. Liquor may assist you with falling sleeping all the more rapidly. In any case, it makes the rest significantly less serene. This is a direct result of liquor impacts on how you process food. It additionally discourages vitality levels. When the liquor has worn off during the night, you'll be bound to wake up. Since remaining productive is connected to getting quality rest, unmistakably maintaining a strategic distance from liquor before bed is a smart thought.

- Setting Up Schedules To Keep Your Day On Target

Setting up sound schedules keeps your day on target and encourages you to remain productive. Making a morning schedule to wake you up and a night schedule that encourages you to loosen up is significant. With an unmistakable example to the day, you'll realize what's coming straightaway. This spares you the time associated with contemplating what to do. It additionally encourages you to feel that you're achieving more in your accessible time.

Productive individuals know about what they should do before the time comes to do it. Recollect that inability to design is intending to fall flat. Make getting ready for the day ahead piece of your night schedule. This will guarantee you have an unmistakable reason and strategic you get up in the first part of the day.

Set your alert early. A great many people perform at their best in the main couple of hours subsequent to getting up (accepting they've had great quality rest). On the off chance that you typically slither up 30 minutes before work starts, change this propensity. Get up at any rate two hours before you go to work. You can utilize this super-productive time to complete more.

Build up an unmistakable night schedule too that advances tranquil rest. Switch off the PC and telephone two or three hours before bed.

Wash up and drink a calming smooth beverage. Take a stab at perusing a book to loosen up you before you at last float off. As we've just brought up, getting adequate great quality rest is basic for productivity.

Plan in any event ten minutes in your day when you do

literally nothing. Regardless of whether you decide to ponder as we referenced before or basically unwind, it'll help clear your mind. With only a short space of time wherein to slow down and never really, improve your general core interest.

Include working out into your day by day schedule. At the point when your body is solid, your mind is sound. Do you think you need adequate time in your day to work out? At that point recollect that you'll perform ten times better when your body and mind profit by the lift in its vitality levels.

Arranging a snooze into your day can likewise do some incredible things. Snoozing for somewhere in the range of 20 and an hour day by day permits your body and mind to rest. During this time, you'll have the option to arrange data in your cerebrum. You'll additionally feel stimulated and prepared to work more earnestly when you wake up.

Every day, plan time in your night calendar to ponder your day. Rewind the happenings in your mind and consider everything that worked out in a good way just as everything that turned out badly. You'll increase supportive experiences and you'll be better ready to devise plans for a superior tomorrow.

Include every one of these components into your day by day

plan and you'll be significantly more productive.

- Distinguish Your Productive Times

Everybody has explicit times of the day when they're generally productive. Maybe for you, it'll be promptly in the first part of the day, or late at night. The key is to distinguish those times. At the point when you've done as such, you can plan your hardest assignments for those hours.

There are, normally, minutes inconsistently when you're progressively engaged, fiery, and productive. At the point when you have to concentrate on a particular errand, it bodes well to plan it for one of those minutes. This will guarantee you apply your earnest attempts to the job that needs to be done.

A great many people have their productive times toward the beginning of the day. The initial two hours in the wake of waking are regularly the best. Be that as it may, this isn't valid for everybody. You should be in line with your body rhythms to distinguish your pinnacle hours.

To do this, you have to focus not on the clock however to your own body. On the off chance that you drive yourself to accomplish your hardest work when you need vitality and center, you'll simply wear out. In this manner, you have to concentrate on transit you feel. Know about when your vitality level is plunging. Proof shows that the human mind needs a break following an hour and a half of working seriously. Know about the signs that your body is sending you. Do you feel languid, nervous? Hungry? Those could be signs you need a brief break.

At the point when you're on top of your productivity bend, you can design your hardest assignments into your most productive window. At that point, what do you do with the rest of your day?

Completing the hardest assignment consistently causes you to feel achieved. Nonetheless, during the rest of your time, you ought to be taking a shot at advancing critical errands. You can likewise make up for lost time with updates, gatherings, and correspondences. Because you aren't at your most productive doesn't mean you ought to complete nothing.

Plan assignments to suit your vitality levels at each phase of the day.

- On the occasion of low vitality levels, plan calls, messages, and gatherings.

- On the occasion of higher vitality, plan pressing work, and day by day assignments.

- At your pinnacle productivity hours, plan to do the

most testing employments.

- At your most reduced vitality level, enjoy a reprieve.

Recollect that investing more energy working doesn't mean you'll essentially complete more work. Quality time is a higher priority than the time span. In this way, plan your concentration to suit your vitality levels and you'll be progressively productive by and large.

CHAPTER FIVE

Relieve Anxiety

Everyone has anxiety in one form or another during their life. From being anxious about a job interview, exam, or medical test. These are normal emotional states.

It is when we struggle to control these worries that it then affects our daily lives. For me and many I have encountered, it is like a downward ever more challenging spiral.

People with anxiety

When I have spoken to people with anxiety, I am amazed how many on the surface you would not expect to have it. How many manage to control it and appear on the outside at least like they are not dealing with anything.

Anxiety has three sides: mental, physical, and emotional. Our self-talk is of worry for the future. Emotionally we feel fearful. Physically we are tense.

Fascinating fact—over 70% of your body's systems are used during your anxiety disorder! This explains why you always feel exhausted!

The most common symptoms can be:

- Headaches/pressure—feels like head about to explode Palpitations

- Dizziness

- Weak legs—feel like jelly Feeling detached from the world Tension and muscle aches Sweating

- Shortness of breath Fatigue and tiredness Increased heart rate Digestive problems

- Irritable

- Mind constantly racing

This can manifest in a variety of other disorders like:

- Phobias

- Panic disorders

- Post-traumatic disorder Social anxiety disorder OCD

So many people these days suffer from one form or another. I used to live being stressed every day. It isn't healthy and burns you out. It also leads to being anxious.

Anxiety is an isolating experience. It's overwhelming. It can damage relationships with family and friends and can threaten people's careers and lives. Many people don't understand how hard and energy-sapping being anxious is.

Anxiety is so complex and individual to that person. There are a lot of different types of anxiety like:

- Social anxiety

- General anxiety (GAD) High-performing anxiety

People can appear to look calm, self-assured, and confident on the outside, but drowning on the inside.

There is no reasoning or logic that can help. Anxiety is purely an emotional state. Most of the time we know what is happening, we understand the logic and battle it, but we feel we have no control over what is happening.

It took me four weeks just to take some rubbish to the local recycling depot. The thought of going made me anxious and fraught with worry. My stomach was in knots. I was scared. It has been one of the few times I couldn't explain why and still don't. I have done it loads of times in the past without problems. This time was different. I had to push myself so hard just to get it done in the end I did it. It only took me 14 minutes to do it. Round trip. I had to listen to Marvel music to inspire me the whole time. Five bags of rubbish!

I felt stupid and ashamed afterward. 'Why the hell did it take you that long? It's only just down the bloody road, you d**k!'

Days have been safer not to write. But I want to make a difference to people. The only way I will is by giving everything. And pushing beyond my fears. To show you exactly what is going on in my head.

Anxiety is generally brought on by negative thoughts and vice-versa. When you dwell on the negatives, anxiety tends to shoot through the roof. Hence, the following strategies will help you get a handle on your negative thoughts thereby curbing your anxiety.

Thought Journals

Thought diaries chip away at a similar reason. They offer you the chance to get outside of your musings and get a progressively target viewpoint on them. First, you identify the substance of your negative musings, and after that, you record them in your diary.

This makes you mindful of your considerations, gets you outside of them and enables you to survey them and choose whether or not they are valid.

Contemplation

Contemplation implies analyzing past, and current, events in order to distill valuable lessons from them. If you simply dwell on how miserable a situation made you feel, then you will only be fueling negative feelings inside of you. So, the next time something negative happens, do not be afraid to sit down and deconstruct why it happened. Then, take the most valuable lessons and put them to good use.

Intellectual Behavioral Therapy and Cognitive Restructuring Psychological rebuilding is a procedure where you identify your negative idea examples and afterward question them. As such, subjective rebuilding is a procedure where you research your negative musings and build up that they are not valid.

There are five phases to intellectual rebuilding:

1. Question - This is exactly what it seems like. Evaluate your negative considerations if you think they are not valid.

2. Challenge them. If you will, in general, think you are a disappointment, review to mind times when you were not a disappointment. If you will, in general, imagine that you are constantly a disappointment in social

circumstances, review to mind events in which you and someone else felt near each other. By and by, this is tied in with figuring out how to quit accepting your negative musings.

3. Identify and Record - The main activity is to identify your negative musings and record them in a diary. Also, record the circumstance where you had every episode of negative contemplations and how the musings made you feel. This will begin the way toward isolating yourself from your negative considerations.

4. Practical Goals - Negative considerations are frequently the handmaiden of having ridiculous pictures of and objectives for yourself. It is possible that you should be extraordinary in all that you do. Or then again you may request that yourself be somebody you aren't. This sort of mental self- view is an arrangement for negative contemplations. You will regularly be a disappointment in your own eyes, and this will offer ascent to negative musings. Create sensible objectives for your work life and your public activity. This will diminish your negative mental self-portraits and negative musings.

5. Positive Thoughts - When negative considerations come up, supplant them with positive contemplations.

"I enjoyed myself at that last gathering I went to". "Last week's gathering, everyone thought my marketable strategy was brilliant, and we utilized the arrangement with a couple of slight modifications."

6. Examine - Analyze the considerations in your idea diary. Search for examples in the subjects of your musings. Do your contemplations make negative pictures of yourself? What are the negative pictures they make? Try to perceive what sorts of circumstances trigger your negative considerations. The vast majority of all, investigate the musings to check whether they are truly valid.

CHAPTER SIX

Understanding Stress

What is Stress?

As humans, a part of our daily life consists of us going through changes. To keep up with these changes, the body must react appropriately. Stress refers to how the body responds to these changes.

It is a means by which the body prepares you for a new situation. This can be emotionally, physically, or mentally. An individual will choose either a fight or flight response in such circumstances.

The stress we experience can either be positive or negative. When stress is positive, then it comes to motivate you, alert, and prepare you for impending danger so you can avoid it. Negative stress usually occurs when there are too many stressors.

The presence of excess stressors will result in tension and

overwork due to stress. This is due to the inability of the body to get any form of rest before the next stressful situation. It can result in distress, which is your reaction to negative stress.

What are Stressors?

Stressors refer to the various situations or events that your body interprets as a threat. These serve as a trigger to the stress response mechanism of the body. In simpler form, they are events that promote stress in your life.

How Does Pressure Influence Stress?

One of the simplest things that you notice from your interaction with other individuals is the fact that you are different in so many ways. These include your speech patterns, hair color, weight, tics, and reactions to similar situations. The same applies when discussing stress.

In this discussion, it is common to bring up the issue of pressure. This is often one of the reasons why some people find themselves experiencing stress. Nonetheless, not everyone will feel the same way.

Pressure for some individuals provides motivation, stimulation, and a drive to complete a task. For another individual, this same level of pressure might produce a higher level of stress hormones in the body. This is where our unique differences play a role.

What this implies is that what you may find to be the optimum level of pressure you need to work effectively and creatively will lead to stress in the life of another person.

This can be in the form of burnout or anxiety. There is also an issue when you are getting below the optimum level of pressure.

This lack of optimum pressure can lead to a situation in which you are depressed, bored, or apathetic. There is a possibility of reaching 'rust out' due to this lack of pressure. Rust out refers to a situation in which you're unable to reach your full potential due to a lack of challenge.

Understanding these two unique situations, burnout, and rust out, it is much easier to differentiate pressure from stress. While pressure can lead to both rust out and burnout, it only results in stress if it is tilting toward the burnout level.

Balancing the level of pressure to suit your optimum level is essential if you want to avoid stress and also prevent the frustration, depression, boredom, or apathy that is present when you're not getting enough challenge.

Types of Stress

There are various types of stress that you can experience.

To a large extent, the effect of stress on your body depends on the type you are experiencing. These are some of the kinds of stress that you can experience:

Chronic Stress

Chronic stress refers to any form of stress that an individual experience continuously for long periods.

If you are experiencing any form of stress that you feel is impossible to escape, then this might be a sign of chronic stress. In several cases, when you fail to resolve acute stress, it can develop into chronic stress.

There are various examples of chronic stress, including an unhealthy marriage, trauma, financial difficulties, an inconvenient job, and so on.

Considering the numerous health issues attributed to stress, chronic stress is a crucial contributor to some of these health issues, including:

- Cirrhosis of the liver Heart diseases Accidents

- Suicide

- Cancer

- Lung diseases

Eustress

This is any form of stress that you experience that provides excitement, fun, or benefit to you. Moments when you experience an increase in adrenaline levels are usually closely related to eustress. An example of such moments is when you are exercising.

Acute Stress

Anytime you experience stress that lasts only a short time is usually acute stress. Both positive and negative stress can fall into the category of acute stress.

When this form of stress occurs at different times, it can provide some benefits to the body.

Situations that promote acute stress usually trigger the fight-or-flight mechanism of the body. This is how the body appropriately responds to any new demand, challenge, or event. Following these situations, the body can develop on the best and most effective response to such cases if it occurs in the future.

A common example of positive acute stress includes getting on a rollercoaster. Negative acute stress can be experienced in situations such as arguments with your spouse or a near-miss accident. Depending on the severity of the acute stress, there may be lasting health issues.

An example of this is noticeable in individuals with post-traumatic stress disorder. These individuals develop this disorder as a result of experiencing a life-threatening situation or a crime.

Episodic Acute Stress

In typical situations, acute stress should be short-term and infrequent. Regardless, there are situations when it becomes regular and a part of the daily life of an individual. In such cases, it becomes episodic acute stress.

These individuals have come to the conclusion that there is a need for stress in their daily life.

Due to this acceptance, changing to a healthier lifestyle is difficult. This form of stress is common in individuals who exhibit anxiety, irritability, and a short temper.

This chaotic lifestyle is also noticeable in pessimistic individuals who are always looking for the negative in every situation.

Health Issues Due to Stress

Your health is your priority when dealing with stress. It may seem insignificant when considering it over a short-term, but long-term exposure to stress will take its toll on your body. There are different ways that this can happen.

Here are some of the common health issues that are associated with stressful situations:

Accelerated Aging

Accelerated aging has always been an issue in discussions regarding stress. To provide facts regarding this issue, there have been various studies and research.

There are several ways through which stress can cause accelerated aging in individuals (Gregoire, 2013):

Damage to Cells

This is due to workplace stress in our lives.

By measuring the telomeres of different individuals, a study was able to determine that those with higher workplace stress levels had shorter telomere. The adverse effects associated with the shortening of the telomeres include cardiovascular diseases, Parkinson's, cancer, and type 2 diabetes.

It Ages the Brain

In another study by UC Berkeley, scientists identified that in females, higher stress levels could promote a rapid brain decline, which is aging-related.

Unhealthy Lifestyle Choices

Your habits have an effect on proper aging. Poor habits like sleep deprivation is a result of stress in your life. Sleep deprivation is one of the factors that promote rapid aging.

It is also common to ignore exercises and don't eat a balanced diet while under stress. These individuals rely more on medications and alcohol. This will surely become noticeable in how the body ages.

It Results in Loss of Vision and Hearing

Another result from research shows that due to the continuous production of adrenaline over time, there is a noticeable constriction of the blood vessels. This constriction can cause a drop in vision and hearing of the individual.

More research is necessary to determine if this decrease is permanent, so we can assume that a temporary hearing and vision loss is possible due to stress.

Diabetes

Diabetes is another health issue that is affected and promoted by stress. In the people suffering from type 1 or type 2 diabetes, they suffer from the effects of physical stress. This form of stress causes a rise in the blood sugar level of the individual.

With mental stress, it might affect individuals with type 1 diabetes differently. For some, there will be an increase in blood glucose levels, while others will experience a decrease. For those with type 2 diabetes, there is also an issue when they are under mental stress. This type of stress results in a rise in the blood glucose level of the individual.

Stress can also promote diabetes. This is noticeable in the increase in the chances of an individual adopting bad behavior. In this case, unhealthy food choices.

They resort to excessive drinking and eating a poor diet. This might also affect those already suffering from this condition.

Depression

Depression is one of the health issues that can result from chronic or acute stress. This situation occurs when the body is unable to shut-down and reset the stress response system after overcoming a stressful situation. A tasking job that offers minimal rewards or the loss of a loved one is one of such events.

Such events result in the reduction of neurotransmitters such as dopamine and serotonin, with an increase in cortisol levels. Due to the inability to shut- down the stress response, the body is unable to return these levels to normal, meaning that the body will be unable to function optimally.

This means there will be a dopamine deficiency in the body, which has a close link to depression in humans (Cadman & Falck, 2018). With lower stress levels, the risk of depression is much lower.

Obesity

Another significant health problem that individuals may experience due to stress is obesity. There have been research with conclusions that prove this to be a fact. In one study, the samples used in determining this risk was the hair cortisol level (Whiteman, 2017).

According to this study, individuals with a higher hair cortisol level also had a heavier weight, bigger waist circumference, and higher body mass index (BMI). In comparison to excess fat in the hips and leg area, excess belly fat poses a more significant health risk.

There is also the issue of "comfort eating," in which

individuals try to make themselves feel better by consuming foods that have high sugar and fat content. This is an action that also promotes obesity, and this "comfort eating" is a result of stress.

Premature Death

If you don't manage stress properly, there is a high risk that it can shorten your lifespan. This includes the everyday stress you experience in life. Through chronic stress, there is a possibility of an increase in blood pressure.

This form of stress also reduces your immunity and affects your memory due to the rise in the level of cortisol in the body. In other situations, your reaction to everyday stress also has a role to play.

Heart Diseases

To establish a direct link between stress and heart diseases, there is a need for in-depth research into this area. Nonetheless, there are other indirect ways by which stress can lead to heart diseases.

There is a possibility of stress leading to heart muscle inflammation. This is one of the areas that play a role in heart diseases. The possibility of causing a sudden jump in your blood pressure is also present with stress.

People who experience stress tend to overeat, smoke, and drink. This is their solution to get over stress, but these actions also increase the risk of heart disease. There is also a risk of heart attack, hypertension, or stroke due to the damage to the blood vessel lining of an individual experiencing chronic stress.

How These Health Issues Adversely Affect Your Family

When you are down with health issues due to stress, you can expect it to have an unwanted effect on your family members. The first comes in need to care for you. The things you could do on your own may no longer be possible.

As a result, you need the assistance of others. This means if the family can't afford a nurse to be by your side at all times, then someone has to be around you.

Another way is the financial setback it causes, no one will be blaming you for your predicament, but the strain on the family finances will show. In addition to spending on treatment, you might not have the opportunity to work as you could before. Not everyone gets to perform at their peak despite battling a health issue.

It is also vital that you note that illnesses will cause a lifestyle change in your family. How it affects each family member will differ. Regardless of how it affects them, there are going to be some changes that they must accept.

CHAPTER SEVEN

Declutter Your Life

We as a whole have a clutter of clutter in our lives. Sometimes, that clutter is physical - records on the work area or heaps of garbage in the home. Different times, it's enthusiastic or mental clutter. Do you generally appear to have a lot to consider? Is it true that you are on edge and worried about the things you haven't cultivated? Do you battle to concentrate on a certain something? Clutter is the guilty party.

Clutter, regardless of whether mental or physical, can genuinely harm your productivity. At the point when you're encircled by clutter, you can't commit yourself to the main job. Records all over your work area make it hard to deal with the one you have to concentrate on. Garbage all over your home makes it difficult to keep on your family unit tasks. Decluttering your life is, consequently, key to remaining productive and accomplishing your own best.

- Clutter – The Foe Of Productivity

A cluttered situation is a disorganized domain. Turmoil impacts contrarily on your core interest. It additionally prevents your cerebrum from appropriately handling data. Clutter diverts you and prevents you from finishing undertakings productively and adequately. On the other hand, a peaceful sorted out and the uncluttered condition is helpful for helping you center.

Why is clutter so hindering to your capacity to center?

At the point when you over-burden the cerebrum, it needs to partition its capacity. This makes it harder to process data and switch between assignments. It likewise impacts on your working memory.

At the point when you're in the working environment, clutter can be incredibly adverse. It can actually keep you from completing your activity. Studies have demonstrated that the normal specialist goes through around 4.3 hours every week simply searching for administrative work. In addition to the fact that this adds dissatisfaction and worry to the workplace, yet it additionally diminishes innovative reasoning and focus.

At the point when your workspace is decluttered, you can be progressively sorted out. You can, in this way, continue higher productivity, remaining completely centered around your needs.

In what manner can you declutter at work? Follow these top tips:

- Receive a viable documenting framework. On the off chance that you permit administrative work to accumulate, you'll simply sit around idly scanning for papers. A precise arrangement of documenting implies you'll realize where everything is the point at which you need it. It will likewise keep things off your work area and in an assigned area.

- Keep your work surfaces as clear as could reasonably be expected. Keep fundamentals like pens or scratchpad inside a safe distance. Keep everything else in drawers or cupboards far out.

- An investigation has shown that Americans squander as long as multi- week every year looking for missing things. Try not to turn into a measurement! Have a spot for everything and keep everything in its place. That way, you'll never be pondering where things are.

- Toward the finish of every workday, give your work

area a redesign. Verify whether any things can be discarded or taken care of. This will assist you with staying on the clutter that heaps up after some time.

Shouldn't something be said about in the home? Clutter in your home prompts clutter in your mind. It's along these lines essential to downplay mess in your living space as well.

How might you diminish the clutter at home? Here are some top tips:

- Be heartless. Try not to keep things since you're sentimental about them. In the event that there's something that has sentimental worth yet isn't valuable, snap a picture of it. You would then be able to dispose of the thing itself and simply show the photograph.

- Set yourself standard times during the time to give things to a noble cause. When a month is a decent objective. Save a crate for this reason and put things in it consistently. At that point, on your picked date, take it to a neighborhood gift focus.

- Consider selling any things you do not utilize anymore or need. Not exclusively will this declutter your home, however it'll likewise make some valuable additional money?

- Try not to look for no particular reason. On the off chance that you really need something, you should just take enough cash to pay for that thing. Try not to shop since you feel discouraged or for an approach to breathe easy. Expel shopping applications from your cell phone. This will assist you with saving cash and will prevent clutter from working up.

- Check what you have and use it. Rather than purchasing new furnishings, give old pieces a makeover with a layer of paint. As opposed to purchasing another outfit, consider how you can repurpose existing garments. Transform destroyed pants into shorts or cut the sleeves off an old coat to make a gilet.

- Consider receiving the time for testing mindset. In case you're reluctant to dispose of a specific thing, store it away for a set period. You'll presumably find that you can undoubtedly oversee without it. At that point, you can dispose of it.

- Embrace the one thing in, one thing out mindset. On the off chance that you get one new thing, dispose of an old thing. This prevents clutter from working up. Rather than a storeroom loaded with shoes, you'll just have the ones you need and wear, for instance.

It's never simple to declutter your life. We as a whole will in general crowd things. Be that as it may, we seldom need the things that mount up in our homes and workspaces. By being heartless, we can limit the physical clutter. This, thusly, causes us to complete more and feel better intellectually as well.

- Take Out Computerized Interruptions

Interruptions aren't all physical. Nowadays, there are a lot of computerized interruptions as well. These can be significantly more unfavorable to productivity than physical ones. Have you at any point wound up looking through Facebook as opposed to dealing with that significant report? It's a very regular issue.

It appears that interruptions are all over the place. From television to web- based life, it's critical to expel them when you have other things to concentrate on. Regardless of whether you're taking a shot at an errand at home or in the workplace, advanced clutter stops your productivity.

How might you dispose of your advanced clutter? Here are some top tips:

- Manage your old messages. To start with, experience your old messages. Erase any which are not, at this point required. For the rest, make envelopes in your inbox where you can store them away. Make one organizer explicitly for things that you have to manage. This will keep them in one advantageous area until you've managed them.

- Handle your inbox. Set up certain guidelines for approaching mail. At whatever point you get spam, withdraw then erase. This will prevent further spam from working up. On the off chance that an email shows up requesting a reaction, tackle it quickly on the off chance that you can answer it in under two minutes. Recollect that 2-minute principle? In the event that it'll take longer, put it into your envelope and tackle it when you can.

- Tackle your downloads. Set a time once every month or every week to experience your downloads envelope. You'll, as a rule, discover you can erase the majority of your downloads. The rest ought to be moved into a proper envelope.

- Compose your organizers. Having envelopes that are

anything but difficult to utilize and get to is critical to productivity. Arrange by need, classification, or date as you see fit. Sort your envelopes on your telephone as well. Gathering your applications into explicit subfolders so they're anything but difficult to track down.

- Reinforcement of your significant reports and data. Regardless of whether you use distributed storage or a physical hard drive, keeping those things in a protected area is foremost.

- Deal with your web-based life. Occasionally, you ought to experience your internet-based life systems and expel anything superfluous or inconsequential. Unfriend, unfollow, and make space for progressively significant life impacts.

- Erase your bookmarks. Bookmarks are valuable when you're managing pages. Be that as it may, ensure you set a time to check the rundown routinely. This permits you to erase any bookmarks that aren't important any longer.

- Erase your perusing history and treats consistently. This will accelerate your PC's beginning uptime and help forestall crashes. This spares you time and causes you to remain productive.

- Utilize an ace secret word application or program. This assists with sparing you the upsetting undertaking of recalling all your logins and passwords. It'll additionally guarantee they remain safe from programmers and cybercriminals.

- Winnow old projects and applications. Set a customary time every month to experience your PC and telephone. Erase any projects or applications you don't utilize or require. This liberates space and speeds things up.

- Manage your photographs. We as a whole take innumerable photographs on our telephones nowadays. In any case, many are pointless. You most likely have six duplicates of the equivalent selfie as you attempted to get the perfect edge! Erase the ones you don'tcare for. Erase any pictures you'll never take a gander at again. The greater part of us has snapped a picture in a store to send a companion to ask their supposition. You needn't bother with those shots any longer, so get free!

At the point when you dispose of advanced clutter just as physical clutter, you'll be increasingly productive.

- Clear Your Mind

In addition to the fact that you need to manage physical and computerized clutter, yet you ought to likewise evacuate mental clutter. Nowadays, we're continually hurrying about. This implies your mind can get cluttered. Thus, this diminishes your productivity since you can't center.

Reflection is a valuable device to destroy this psychological clutter. It likewise causes you to accomplish more noteworthy clearness. You can enjoy a psychological reprieve from the worries of regular day to day existence.

You'll additionally be better ready to tune into yourself.

In the event that you haven't reflected previously, you may need to rehearse for some time before you get the thought. Start gradually to slide yourself into the training delicately. Locate an agreeable, calm spot where you're ready to unwind. Start with just a short, 10-minute meeting.

Contemplation is a device you use to turn out to be increasingly mindful. You center around both your body and your breath. On the off chance that you discover your mind meandering, essentially recognize it and take it back to your relaxing.

Contemplation doesn't simply help clear your mind; it additionally diminishes your feeling of anxiety. This assists in boosting your core interest.

Subsequently, you can turn out to be increasingly productive and accomplish your own best.

Is it true that you are prepared to start thinking?

- Locate an agreeable spot that is quiet and calm.

- Set a breaking point on your reflection time – around 10 minutes is a decent spot to begin.

- Put your center onto your body. You can stoop, sit on a seat or on the floor. Ensure you're agreeable and stable.

- Concentrate on your relaxing. Feel yourself take in and out.

- Try not to pass judgment on yourself brutally if your mind meanders. Simply return it to your relaxing. It's typical for your mind to meander from the outset.

- When the assigned time is done, gradually open your eyes. Put in almost no time getting increasingly mindful of where you are and how you feel. Notice your sentiments and feelings.

Practice every day, gradually expanding the time allotment you spend reflecting. Before long, you'll see it simpler to declutter your mind of meddling contemplations that keep you from being productive.

CHAPTER EIGHT

Self-Improvement

Ways You Can Improve Your Life

It does not have to be just performing one major thing to change your life. Rather, it is something you should focus on constantly — and usually, it is down to the small tasks you do daily.

I recognize that while there is a job, families, and expenses to pay, no one in the universe has all the energy to dream about self-improvement and personal growth, so let us continue with only 30 minutes a week.

Yes, that's it... I believe you are listening to now.

What I am asking is for you to pursue one (or two, or five, or all) of these practices to see whether they can enable you to become a stronger "you," if that means raising your trust, reducing your depression, building deeper relationships or being a healthier person.

Achieve Mindfulness

I am sure you are so sick to learn that you should "consider meditation altogether," particularly from your (recently) yoga-crazed mom. However, to gain consciousness is far more practical than the type of therapy you read of, as it doesn't take years of preparation and a yoga pad. And, even sitting there at your office takes 30 minutes (or less!).

Let Go of Anger

We are all getting angry with our lives. However, the unchecked rage will trigger issues in our relationships, and in our wellbeing. All this will contribute to more pressures and extra issues, which will render things more difficult and keep us from becoming our best selves. This is why it is so necessary to know how to handle and finally let go of frustration and become a stronger individual.

Letting go of frustration isn't always simple, so thinking something about understanding rage and realizing what to do when you get upset about your life is the first phase about anger management.

Recognizing frustration is also easy if you make an effort to acknowledge when you are angry and try to handle the emotion rather than ignore it or strike out at people as a means to cope.

Reflect on knowing why you are feeling upset and why and realize there is a distinction between feeling angry and acting on the frustration. Know then your choices.

You should adjust your own opinions about what makes you mad. This will help by thinking all about the case, or by telling yourself that there may be stuff, you do not already recognize.

Remember, perhaps that person who cut you off in traffic has been interrupted in their own lives by something daunting.

If a friend appears disrespectful to you, inquire how their day is going and figure out if there's anything you don't hear about.

You should also concentrate on what are the "pain causes" and remove them as soon as you can. For starters, if you get stressed and upset because you need to hurry, focus on having more room in your life (even if it means saying no more), and seek to remove the cause. If a certain person gets you upset, then try to limit their role in your life if it does not function first to talk things out.

It is also important to learn how to let go of daily grudges and lingering rage. Do not wake up from the night before holding a grudge, if you can stop. Reflect on redemption, even if it means you still do not let your life play a significant role. Remain as much as possible in the present moment, and that becomes simpler.

They can also help to let go of frustration by using tension relievers such as yoga—Focus on removing the impact that the past might have on you. Put your mind to the moment to stop ruminations from living in a pleasant position.

Support Others

Helping others would sound like an easy path to becoming a better individual, so we always think of "healthy people" as someone able to give for others. That is what makes an individual "healthy" in the eyes of others. Nevertheless, good actions will often make us happier people because of the connection between altruism and emotional health.

According to the study, it might always be accurate that giving is greater than receiving. So, when you may be too overwhelmed and distracted thinking about your own and your family's issues to extend your support to others when it is not necessary, extending your capacity to concentrate on other people's needs will also improve. It is true: altruism is a benefit of its own, which will potentially help alleviate tension.

Research suggests that altruism is beneficial for your mental well-being, which will improve your state of mind measurably.

For instance, one analysis showed that patients with dialysis, transplant patients, and family members who were volunteers to help other patients reported improved professional development and emotional health.

One research on patients with multiple sclerosis (MS) found that people who gave social help to other MS patients significantly reported greater benefits than their sponsored peers, including more marked trust gain, self-awareness, self-esteem, stress, and day-to-day functioning.

In addition to making the planet a healthier environment, you will become a happier, more caring human by practicing your altruism. While there are so many forms of communicating altruism, there is a straightforward approach to be a better human, one that is open to us all every day. It is also a positive fortune.

Leverage Your Strengths

Losing track of time when you are involved in doing a job or other stimulating task, or what psychologist's term "flow," is a common phenomenon for most of us.

Flow is what occurs when you get actively interested in a sport, acquiring new talent or topic, or participating in activities that offer just the right balance of difficulty and ease. (When we feel too overwhelmed, we feel frustrated, and when things are too simple, we can get distracted–either way, reaching the perfect spot between these two extremes keeps us involved in a perfect way).

You can encounter flow by writing, acting, making, or learning new content that you may teach others. To some, what will get you to the condition of being can be daunting, and vice versa. Think of where you most frequently find yourself in this environment and seek to do some of that.

The flow condition is a strong predictor of whether an operation is correct for you.

You harness your talents while you are in a state of relaxation, and that works out to be perfect for your mental wellbeing and satisfaction. It is actually a good idea about the people of the planet, as you will typically use your talents to support someone in any way.

Once you think enough about yourself to recognize what are your strongest qualities and figure out how to leverage them for the good of others, you are on your way to become a stronger individual, and therefore a happy one. Using what you are strong at and build a flow state that is how to point in the right direction.

Use the "Stages of Change" Model

If you had a magic wand, ask yourself, what would you want to see appear in the future? Ignoring the thoughts about how you are supposed to get there, you will easily picture your dream future, and what is included in it.

Take a few minutes to list the improvements and priorities that will be included in this picture, on paper, or on your screen. Be clear about what you desire. It is all right if you like something you obviously have no power over or a friend that is ideal for you. Only write it down.

You may follow the example of other companies and have a timeline for your

existence spanning one year, five years, and ten years. (It does not have to be a set-in-stone dream, just a list of hopes and objectives.)

Having in mind what you're aiming for in the future will make you become less lost in the difficult areas of your daily life, and let you find more opportunities for improvement as they daily themselves.

There are many avenues to concentrate on transition, but the progress model phases will maybe take you to your true selves more quickly than several other directions.

The shift approach can be adapted to any mentality you have right now, which will function with most people.

Some of the most critical aspects of this path to progress are that you don't force yourself to make adjustments until you're ready, and you don't give up if you catch yourself backsliding — it's a part of the transition cycle that is forgivable and often anticipated. Comprehending this improvement strategy will motivate you to be a happier individual in any way you want.

Take Care of Yourself

You may not always be in charge of the situations you encounter, but you may be able to control how well you take care of yourself, which can influence your stress levels and enable you to grow as a person while confronted with the challenges of life.

For many factors, self-care is essential to creating resistance while faced with such inevitable stressors. You will also be more sensitive to the pressures you encounter in your life when you are too stressed, eating badly, or just run- down. Even by behaving badly rather than working from a position of relaxed inner strength, you may end up creating more issues for yourself.

In comparison, when you take good care of yourself (both your body and mind), you can be more thoughtfully involved with anything that arrives, use the opportunities that you have in your life, and really learn from the obstacles that you encounter, rather than just enduring them.

Taking careful care of your body, soul and mind will keep you in good condition to handle stress, which gives you additional endurance to tackle the struggles we all face in life, as well as those which may be special to you.

For your emotional and physical well-being, sleep is important because too little or poor-quality sleep will make you feel more anxious and less likely to find solutions to problems that you face. Lack of sleep can also take a toll on your body, both in the short and long term. Bad sleep may also have an effect on your weight.

The same holds true with poor nutrition. Moreover, a bad diet will also lead you to feel overweight and exhausted and can accumulate additional pounds over time. You need the right nutrition to tackle the struggles of life, but when depression hits, it is always the junk food that we want.

Feeling related to others will make you become more responsive to any obstacles that you encounter. Good friends will help you handle negative emotions, create ideas, and, when appropriate, get your mind off your problems. It is also difficult to find time for friends when you are experiencing a crazy, exhausting life, but through their encouragement and motivation, our friends also make us better people.

It is important to take some time for yourself, eventually. This may involve journaling and reflection, whether that may come in the form of exercising or sometimes viewing home reruns. This is particularly relevant for introverts, but everybody requires some time for themselves, often at least.

Learn to Be User-Friendly

The partnerships will build a refuge from pain, and at the same time, motivate us to become better people. Often, they may be a major cause of tension when disagreement is badly handled or left to fester. The strength of that is that it will still be a road to become a stronger human because we do the research it takes to become a stronger spouse, wife, and family member.

One of the stuff you should do both to strengthen your partnerships and to better yourself is to study techniques for dispute resolution. Being a strong listener, respecting the other hand while you are in disagreement, and developing strategies for controlling frustration.

These things will help us become healthier versions of ourselves. They may also alleviate the tension in the relationships we encounter and make them stronger. Yet near partnerships typically provide many chances to exercise these skills when you are trying to develop them, and you may enjoy the occasions as they emerge and be less frustrated.

Get Outside

Remember how I did not tell "go-to workout" or "go for a sprint." In addition, yeah, it's fun to exercise. Nevertheless, it is far easier said than done for most men, including myself.

Now, I have another alternative for you — go outside. Walk around, sit down and read in the park, or take a leisurely bike ride. In so many respects, even getting outside is healthy for you. This stimulates imagination, lets us age better, keeps us healthier, and may actually make you want to do more research (science says so!).

CHAPTER NINE

Realizing The Issues

See, you're a brilliant person. An inventive person. A devoted person. I'm quite sure pretty much the entirety of that, or you wouldn't be an aspiring visionary or perusing this digital book. Things being what they are, why you can't resolve a little procrastination issue?

In case you're similar to many individuals, that question has frequented you for quite a while. Among the most disappointing things about procrastination is that it seems like it would be the easiest issue on the planet to determine.

As a matter of fact, it's among the hardest. Extremely, that is not exactly evident. Any issue is hard to fathom in case you're not really understanding it.

I mean it: the best way to determine an issue is to determine it. On the off chance that you endeavor to determine an issue using activities intended to determine some other issue, or activities intended to determine no issue by any means, yet rather to keep up the norm, at that point will undoubtedly bomb. You may attempt from here to the moon, getting control over all the psychological limit, imagination, and enthusiasm you may assemble, you'll still never resolve the issue.

Headed straight toward Fixing It

You likely accept the root issue causing your procrastination is lethargy, absence of order, absence of restraint, youthfulness, absence of duty, or some comparative character imperfection. Be that as it may, learn to expect the unexpected. It's presumably none of those.

Initially, most slackers are not, I rehash, not languid, disorderly, and so on. Indeed, generally will, in general, be dynamos in zones other than the one they're dawdling in. Among the particular miseries of procrastination is that we're much of the time productive in aspects of our lives other than the one nearest to our heart.

Also applying harming marks like "sluggish" or "wayward" to yourself is, from a critical thinking point of view, more terrible than useless. Not exclusively do those names misidentify the issue, they truly exacerbate things by undermining your confidence and inclining you to disappointment.

In addition, individuals habitually live up or down to the marks; so that in the event that someone over and again calls you, or you more than once call yourself, apathetic or uncertain, you're probably going to live "down" to that name.

As a general rule, comprehending, or settling, an issue is a fairly trifling activity when we comprehend what the issue is. Regarding procrastination as a side effect of sluggishness or an absence of control doesn't work, as those are not the reasons for procrastination. Rather, their side effects, much the same as procrastination itself is a manifestation, of a more profound issue.

That issue is regularly either:

You were never shown the propensities for productive work. As we live in a vacuum, this conceivable method you've rather taken in the "default" propensities for low productivity or non-productivity.

This outcome is what I call Conduct Based Procrastination. Or on the other hand, dread: of progress, achievement, disappointment, and so on.

This outcome is what I call Fear-Based Procrastination.

Every now and again, people experience the ill effects of

both.

Conduct Based Procrastination is a nearly simple issue to characterize and comprehend.

Fear-Based Procrastination is increasingly mind-boggling. Not at all like Conduct Based Procrastination, which is ordinarily brought about by an absence of information or preparing, fear Based Procrastination is brought about by, as its name suggests, concern.

Fear is sadly a significant power in many individuals' lives: it's every now and again judicious, if not ideal, response to the difficulties and worries of life and an aspiring way.

Examine the manners in which you can keep catastrophes from occurring.

Produce Plots That Work

To improve the use of your time in your self-start venture, produce plots that stream and function admirably inside your workspace. Arrange and sort out stuff so that a method drives one stage to work with the following stage, etc, etc. Try not to start over each time you need to deliver something.

Produce Plans To Address Dull Employments

This would incorporate any paper and additional advanced

innovation that you'd use to take care of business in your business. Everlastingly have enough supplies accessible that you can promptly get at.

Use a schedule, computerized, or paper, to monitor arrangements. You can perceive what, where, and when you need to do what consistently, initially. This may help you effectively plan your day for ideal outcomes.

Everlastingly work with a spotless work area, with papers recorded and sorted out, and always have the most every now and again used things for your business in your prompt handle.

Plan Enough Rest Periods

Rest specialists suggest for the ordinary, sound adult to get at any rate eight hours of rest a night. This causes them to work adequately and be extremely productive, yet a survey by the National Rest Establishment's 2000 Rest in America omnibus survey found that, by and large, adults rest just shy of seven hours during the week's worth of work.

As a venture, you should plan an adequate measure of rest for ideal productivity. The sum is distinctive for every one of us and you should let your body see what conditions it works best under.

Some require 8 hours, some more, others less. Your body

perceives the appropriate response.

Detail Your Conveying Abilities

Your capacity to apply and certainly convey what you comprehend both orally and recorded as a hard copy is incredibly pivotal to your business' prosperity. Gain it an in-ground promise to keep on bettering your talking and composing aptitudes. You'll spare time and have a progressively effective occupation.

CHAPTER TEN

How To Stop Overthinking

A cluttered mind has no space for anything new. Often, when you feel that your mind is in a state of overdrive, it prevents you from enjoying the opportunities that life has to offer. Overthinking will put you in a constant loop since you feel like you cannot stop yourself from ruminating over a certain issue. The worst thing about this is that there is minimal action you can take to solve the challenge that you are experiencing. As a result, overthinking only damages you as it holds you back from living your life to the fullest.

Learn to be Aware

Just like any other problem that you might be going through, the best way of solving it is by understanding the causes of the problem in the first place. With regard to overthinking, the first step towards dealing with it is by recognizing that you are overthinking. It is important that you live consciously by knowing what is happening in your mind. Any time you feel overwhelmed and stressed, you should take a moment to analyze the situation that you are going through. Your awareness should denote to you that these thoughts roaming in your mind are not helpful. Enhancing your level of self-awareness will help you stop yourself from thinking too much.

The following pointers should help you to boost your self-awareness. Meditate

Today, millions of people value the importance of meditation. Usually, meditation stresses on the aspect of focusing on a certain mantra or your breathing. Meditating regularly increases your self-awareness since you connect with your inner-self in ways that you haven't done before. Meditation will help you connect with your inner self. Accordingly, practicing self-talk keeps you motivated on the goals that you have set for yourself.

Know Your Strengths and Weaknesses

Another effective way of increasing your self-awareness is by knowing your strengths and coping with your weaknesses. Undeniably, as humans we are not perfect. The strengths and weaknesses that we have affect how we work towards our goals. In this regard, most people will only focus on doing the things that they are good at while doing their best to ignore their weaknesses. Knowing yourself better ensures that you don't waste your time and energy doing activities that will only make you feel negatively about yourself.

Know Your Emotional Triggers

In addition, it is essential that you know the emotional triggers that frequently influence your reactions. By knowing these triggers, you can catch yourself before overreacting. Moreover, your self-awareness can be helpful here as it guarantees that your emotions do not overwhelm you. Instead of reacting without thinking twice, you can stop to mull over a particular scenario and act accordingly.

Practice Self-Discipline

Every day, your life will revolve around things that you wish to accomplish. Achieving set goals can be a very positive experience. However, this doesn't come easily. You have to be willing to pay the price. This means that you should learn how to effectively control yourself and focus on what's more important. This is what self-discipline is all about. You should be ready to do anything that brings you closer to your goals.

Try New Experiences

There is a lot that you can gain from life when you learn to value the importance of new experiences. Think about it this way - the more you know, the more you find different ways of approaching life and solving the problems you are facing. Don't limit yourself by going through life with the same perceptions and doing the same things over and over again.

Frankly, this will make every aspect of your life boring. So, go out and have fun. Try new things and challenges.

Motivate Yourself

We all need motivation at some point in life. When you are motivated to do something, your mind has the energy it needs to see through a particular challenge. Therefore, motivation warrants that you embrace positivity in spite of the problems that you might be going through. Indeed, this also has an impact on your self-awareness since you are surer about yourself and your abilities.

Get a Second Opinion

Earlier on, we had pointed out the fact that overthinking can be caused by overcommitting yourself. Maybe this is something that you are accustomed to. We all know how it feels when you manage to successfully complete a project on your own. However, at times it is important to recognize that you can't do everything alone. As you might have heard, "two heads are better than one." Save yourself from the nightmare of weighing your options on something over and over again. Just ask someone else for a second opinion. You will be surprised that you can easily solve a problem that once appeared too difficult for you. Therapy works in the same manner since you get an opportunity to talk over your thoughts with an expert.

Stay Positive

When you are constantly worried that something could go wrong, your mind will race through varying thoughts trying to figure out the best possible solution to solve your situation. Instead of paying too much attention to the negative, change your thoughts and reflect on all the good things that can happen to you. Savor these moments and help your mind adjust to the fact that you can also be happy. Develop a habit of encouraging your thoughts to stay positive.

Identify Distractions

There is a common phrase that goes "what you resist persists." In line with the habit of overthinking, trying to prevent yourself from thinking about something only makes you think too much about it. As a result, the best way of stopping this is by doing something more engaging. Go for a walk with friends. Learn to play a new musical instrument. The point here is that you should make an effort to distract your mind.

Stop Being a Perfectionist

Evidently, there is a good feeling that comes with knowing that you have done something perfectly. Nevertheless, it is quite demanding to do things perfectly all the time. In your everyday life, you should leave room for mistakes. This ascertains that you will not be frustrated when something goes wrong. Focus on learning from your mistakes. Ultimately, you will notice that you start paying less attention to doing things perfectly. This creates room for more opportunities since you will be willing to try anything, whether you succeed or not.

Set Deadlines

Spending too much time thinking about a decision can lead to overthinking. Some decisions do not require you to think too much about them. They are simple choices that you can make within a short period. Therefore, it makes sense to set deadlines that you will make a specific decision before the end of the day. Depending on the importance of the decision, you should set ample time to ensure you end up making sound decisions. Surround Yourself with the Right People At times, it is difficult to think positively if the people you surround yourself with frequently have negative thoughts. If you spend most of your time with people who are always worrying, then you can be sure that you will also find yourself worrying. On the contrary, if you surround yourself with people who always think positively, you will also be influenced to have this perception about your dreams and aspirations. Therefore, you can help stop overthinking by choosing to spend time with productive and positive people. They will help free your mind from worrying about what the future holds for you. With their positive energy, you will appreciate the importance of living in the present.

Do Your Best

When facing new challenges in life, it is a common thing to see most people worry about what they can and cannot do. Unfortunately, this worrying attitude prevents people from handling challenging situations effectively. When faced with difficult situations, it is imperative to focus on giving it your best without thinking too much as to whether you got it right or not. You never know, there are certain situations when the outcome is not as important as you thought.

Create a To-Do List

We can attest to the fact that there are instances when the mind tends to blow things out of proportion. Have you ever heard your inner voice try and convince you that you cannot complete a certain project within a specified period of time?

Frankly, this happens many times where the mind jumps to the conclusion that you have more things to do than you actually do. The funny thing is that the mind will even go to the extent of giving you reasons why you cannot complete the project. To prevent this from happening, you should learn how to work using a to-do list. A to-do list keeps things organized. It guarantees that you can handle one task at a time without making it seem too burdensome for your mind to tackle.

Cut Yourself Some Slack

The desire to succeed might be too ingrained in you that you cannot think of anything else that is not related to what you want. This leads to a scenario where you are too hard on yourself. You will find it difficult to forgive yourself for the little mistakes that you make along the way. Unfortunately, this leads to overthinking.

The truth is that you can't always expect that things will go your way. We are human beings and therefore, we are prone to making mistakes. Successful people understand the importance of making mistakes. It gives them an opportunity to identify their weaknesses and work on them before reaching their goals. Imagine if people only succeeded without making mistakes. Mistakes should be perceived as a stepping stone towards success. As such, always remember that being too hard on yourself is damaging.

On a final note on how to stop overthinking, you should bear in mind that anyone can be a victim of overthinking. We all yearn for the best in life. Therefore, it is okay to overthink things from time to time. However, this becomes a problem when it develops into a habit and you feel as though you cannot do anything about it. Your self-awareness, for example, will come handy each time you slip into a state of overthinking.

Additionally, looking for positive distractions can encourage your mind to think about other things instead of sinking into your thoughts. More importantly, you should always remember to seek a second opinion from those around you. There is a good reason why we have friends and social circles. They should be there to help you offload thoughts and emotions that seem to weigh you down. Talk to your loved ones and if there is no one to talk to, you can always engage in self-talk.

CHAPTER ELEVEN

Specify Your Objectives And Arrange

There are a lot of dependable techniques that are accessible to the exercise of distinguishing and sorting out objectives. Having the option to have a set the plan set up is the first means to guaranteeing achievement in quite a while most noteworthy rate conceivable.

In this way understanding and afterward making an arrangement towards the possible effective culmination of an objective is a significant and profitable exercise to leave upon. Coming up next are only a few suggestions to this end:

Get Going

Setting out the subtleties of the objectives ought to be the initial step to seeing its finishing. When there are away from all the extraordinary parts of the activity set up the individual is better ready to sort out the different activities associated with the procedure.

At that point, there are the need records that ought to be drawn up. These would require the person to recognize and organize the different various parts of the entire exercise as per its significance in connection to keeping the general progression of the undertaking smooth and on track consistently.

Organizer management is one instrument that many have discovered helpful while setting out on a venture that requires the coordination of different connective components.

Archiving and putting away any kind of information in the significant envelopes will guarantee the said information is effectively accessible and available to a second's notification. Disarray and postponements can without much of a stretch be maintained a strategic distance from if this the technique is executed and tenaciously rehearsed.

Keep exacting observing of every single due date is significant, as the proficient running of any undertaking relies upon this. When due dates are not paid attention to there will be an absence of direness to have undertakings finished, which thusly will disturb the general progression of the undertaking.

Having a periodical check and parity list set up is additionally another approach to guarantee the objectives are met in an efficient manner. These periodical checks will help all worried to screen the general by and large advancement and address any regions that need consideration right away.

HAVE A CAN-DO MINDSET

For a huge part of society, things don't come simple and there are no "free" present every step of the way, in this manner the should be solid and embrace the "can do" demeanor at an early stage throughout everyday life.

Change Your Reasoning

With this inspirational disposition solidly set up, not many hindrances can represent the issue as the individual will have the option to take a gander at it in an increasingly positive light. Having a can-do mindset takes practice and persistence, and it isn't difficult to embrace. A portion of the apparatuses to help develop this inspirational mindset is as per the following:

- Consistently have a sound proportion of confidence both in the undertaking being investigated and in one's own ability. This is maybe the most significant fixing to guarantee any fruitful experience. This confidence will see the person through when things appear troublesome and disappointment look conceivable.

- Being as learned as conceivable will likewise contribute decidedly to this psychological go-getting perspective. At the point when one is proficient, handling various errands and encounters won't be overwhelming and have a preferred position that no one but information can Give.

- Being a determined worker additionally implies that bashfulness isn't a piece of one's character. Being bashful will hose any endeavors to be available to openings, in this way, ought to endeavor to keep this specific character quality well leveled out.

- Taking a gander at the part is additionally suggested when one is seeking after victory. This doesn't really mean dressing extravagantly or having costly adornments or toys. It essentially implies showing the certainty that is expected to guarantee different gatherings are sufficiently dazzled to unwind and acknowledge one's perspective on whatever is being talked about.

- Figure out how to "stunning" individuals with your character and information without falling off clumsy or self-important. This is a craftsmanship that when polished to refinement, can empower the requesting of nearly anything from anybody.